A Comprehensive
SUMMARY OF THE BOOK
12 RULES
FOR LIFE

An Antidote To Chaos

BY JORDAN B. PETERSON

**Proudly Brought To You By
James Harvard**

With key points & Key take away

Copyright © 2018; By James Harvard.

Disclaimer

This book is a summary and meant to be a great companionship to the original book or to simply help you get the gist of the original book. If you're looking for the original book, kindly go to Amazon website, and search for 12 Rules for life by Jordan B. Peterson.

Table of Contents

EXECUTIVE SUMMARY

Jordan B. Peterson's "12 Rules for Life" is quite the thought-provoking read. The Canadian clinical psychologist puts forth his ideas about personality, being, existence; the interconnectedness of order and chaos, two forces evident in all of life; the gender roles assignment discourse; the source of the world's greatest evils, and many other controversial topics.

It is refreshing, and sometimes confusing, how he weaves biblical accounts and characters into the telling of his stories. But what might raise the hairs of most are his views on political correctness regarding postmodernism, white-privilege, cultural appropriation and everything in between. One thing is clear about Peterson. He is a man unapologetic of his views, which are largely unpopular, closely conservative, and politically incorrect.

Whichever way it rubs off on you, this is one of those books you cannot forget in a hurry.

RULE 1: STAND UP STRAIGHT WITH YOUR SHOULDERS BACK

KEY TAKEAWAYS:

- *Territory is linked to social status*

- *Every society has people that are in the top rung and those at the bottom*

- *We have the willpower to overcome uncontrollable circumstances and place ourselves in our desired position*

- *A person's posture goes a long way in determining the person's position*

Lobsters tell a lot about the realities of human life; how it works. These crustaceans, easily overlooked, are highly territorial beings and they have a definite structure of status conferral that is quite similar to the world in general. Lobsters live at the bottom of the ocean where each one carves out its own space, or territory. Much like the rest of the world, they have the problem of scarce resources. This leads to a survival-of-the-fittest situation where two lobsters have to fight over ownership of a territory, one eventually coming out as winner and the other, the loser. The status of either winner or loser goes on to determine the amount and quality of resources available to each, and this in turn, dictates the quality of life. This equation is not different from what obtains in the existence of every specie.

In the event that two Lobsters have to fight over one territory, there exists a defensive system programmed into the nervous system of each. They can adopt a particular physical stance that communicates a ready to defend. This mainly involves the opening and raising of their claws. They can also attack their opponent by spraying a liquid from under their eyes. The liquid contains chemicals that send signals about one opponent's size, sex, health, and mood, to the other. Depending on the physical and psychological attributes of both lobsters, a basic display of claws or liquid spray is enough to decide the fate of each, but in an instance that the contenders are similar- in size, strength, confidence, etc.- it degenerates into a full-blown fight where the loser often ends up damaged for life, or worse, dead. The winner goes on to get the best food, the best protection from danger, all the girls, and basically everything at the top of the ladder. In much the same way, territory matters in the human world as well, and often determines social status; where only a small percentage of the entire population occupies the top rung- financially, intellectually, emotionally, physically, psychologically, etc.

A winning lobster usually has a different posture from the loser. The former flexes its appendages such that it looks taller and more terrifying. The latter assumes a hunched, defeated posture. This posture difference is regulated by two chemicals within the lobster neurons- Serotonin and Octopamine. Serotonin induces feelings of confidence while Octopamine produces a cringing personality. Interestingly, winning increases production of Serotonin while losing increases secretion of Octopamine. In this complex equation, a winner is likely to keep on winning and a loser is likely to keep on losing.

This model is useful in explaining the dynamics of territory and social status in human beings. Every society has people that are in the top rung and those at the bottom. For those who find themselves at the top, they have a healthy dose of self-esteem, their pick of the best mates, the best housing, the best nutrition which reduces chances of falling ill and dying early, the best financial opportunities and the expertise to maximise the same. The opposite obtains for people of lower status.

Belonging to either category, often times, is not deliberate. Sometimes, people assume a particular status because of their physical attributes- a slight frame or some form of disability- or psychological feature- a conviction that any form of anger is morally wrong might make an individual prime target for bullying. The brain works in such a way that secretion of either Serotonin or Octopamine is regulated by which of the categories a person tilts most towards, and just as with the lobsters, continued expression of specific attributes increase or decrease production of both chemicals. It all works as part of a mechanism called the feedback loop. It occurs when the reward gotten from a behaviour- invincibility from cocaine, feelings of righteousness after refusing to respond to bullying- induces more of that behaviour. This ends up perpetuating a winning or losing streak.

But we have the ability to turn negatives into positives for ourselves. One of the things you can work at is your body posture. If you have body language that implies defeat or weakness, people are likely to take you as such and relate with you on that basis. On the other hand, adopting a confident, winning stance tends to communicate to yourself and any observer that you know what you're about. It influences the way people relate with you, and being taken seriously and as a person of importance makes you feel better, increasing Serotonin secretion, which in turn, helps you to win some more.

RULE 2 TREAT YOURSELF LIKE SOMEONE YOU ARE RESPONSIBLE FOR HELPING

KEY TAKEAWAYS:

- *We have an innate tendency to self-loathe which dates back to the fall of man in the Garden of Eden*

- *Just as somewhere inside us lies the guilt for the actions of our forefathers, we also retain a consciousness of our initial state of innocence and perfection*

- *We must accept and love the sinners we are while pardoning and supporting other imperfect beings as ourselves*

Human beings would rather take great care of their dogs or cats than take their medication as prescribed by the doctor. This is a baffling thing indeed, but the reason can be traced to the biblical account of creation in the book of Genesis. This theory hinges not on scientific explanation, which only became a form of understanding reality about five hundred years ago, but on something that existed way before science, subjective experience. The latter is characterised by the interaction of crucial elements- Order; Chaos; and the Consciousness that regulates between both. Order is simply familiar territory; everything that is considered normal- buses running on schedule, your kids going to school five days a week, tribe, religion, etc. Chaos is everything unfamiliar that breaks into your familiar world- a sudden ailment assaulting your hitherto perfect body, your spouse cheating on you, a new boss at work, etc. A perpetuation of either Order or Chaos is not natural for any society, which is why both co-exist in our world and our brains have developed a hypersensitivity towards chaos, producing instant reactions.

Tracing it back to our first parents- Adam and Eve- the Genesis account relays how they were created without any form of consciousness; how God gave them a decree not to eat of a particular tree. The serpent- a symbolism for Satan or evil forces in today's world- however convinces her that she will become like God if she ate it. She did, and because no conscious woman wants a man without vision, fed some of it to her man. The serpent left out the part that they would only become like God in the sense that they would now know the difference between good and evil; their inner eyes would be opened. Upon realizing that they were naked, they hid themselves from God, ashamed. This shame and self-contempt is what has been passed down to us in modern times. Unlike animals, who can kill other animals and not be held accountable for their actions because it's their nature, human beings can do bad things with the consciousness that it is bad. We can hurt others just for the sake of hurting them. This ability heightens our self-loathing, which heightens an innate reasoning: why should I help anyone, myself inclusive, capable of such evil?

But just as somewhere inside us lies the guilt for the actions of our forefathers, so do we retain a consciousness of our initial state of innocence and perfection. Just as we take responsibility for our pets, we must begin to take responsibility for ourselves; looking beyond the consciousness of our fallen state and acknowledging the good in us. All around us, there are people who, despite the circumstances, activate their capacity to do good and walk with God again. In my clinical practice, I come across people who I always encourage to appreciate the good in them; the good that they do as well as appreciating it in other people.

We must accept and love the sinners we are while pardoning and supporting other imperfect beings as ourselves. You need to respect and look out for yourself. Reflect on who you really are and identify what is good- and what is not- for yourself. Being proactive about improving the quality of your life- becoming responsible for helping yourself- gives your life a meaning that will compensate for your shame and self-consciousness at your fallen state. It signifies that you can look, with confidence, beyond your sinful nature and learn to commune with God again.

RULE 3 MAKE FRIENDS WITH PEOPLE WHO WANT THE BEST FOR YOU

KEY TAKEAWAYS:

- *Sometimes people make friends with the wrong persons because it makes them look good*

- *Be careful who you make friends with*

- *Not everyone who is down is ready to accept help*

- *Avoid company that pulls you down*

- *It is easier to be bad than be good*

Fairview, Alberta, the town in which I grew up, was a small one. It was a long way from any major city and lacked urban trappings like Cable TV and Internet. Keeping entertained was a task, especially in the five winter months that were so terrible. Drunks passed out on the streets and froze to death, cats lost their ears and

19

tails to frostbite, eyelashes and hair froze, and chimneys and cars lost their function. Fairview was not the most interesting place for young people, but it was worse in winter, and one's friends mattered a lot then.

I had a friend, Chris, who was a very bright lad, but for some reason, confused about life and almost resentful of his near-perfect family. He had a 1972 blue Ford pickup truck that had more dents than body parts, and each time he crashed his truck, his father would fix it and buy him something else. Chris had a cousin, Ed, who was also bright but just as confused as Chris. It didn't help that they both took to Marijuana. We would pass those long nights by either driving from one end of the town to another, or crashing a party.

I never liked being at any of the parties, and neither did most people who eventually left Fairview. The parties were basically filled with teenagers wasting their lives by engaging in highly unprofitable activities- excessive smoking and drinking and daredevil stunts by drunk or high teenagers. Later in high school after most of my friends had dropped out, I made friends with two newcomers who were very different. They were very ambitious but easy to relate with none the same. One would later become my college roommate and we would go on to make an enviable name for ourselves in the institution.

Moving away from Fairview gave me a better perspective on life. I was in a new place, experiencing new opportunities, and knowing I could make the most of them. But unfortunately, not everyone pans out this way. Much later on, I moved to Edmonton with my sister and invited Ed to our place. He was worse than I had last seen him; looking every inch the Marijuana user and taking menial jobs that were not befitting of his intelligent personality. Chris eventually had committed suicide after years of almost going insane.

Why do people like Chris or Ed keep choosing people and places that are not good for them? Sometimes when people have a low self-worth, they tend to be attracted to others that they believe are the same; the lowest of the low. Sometimes also, people stay with the wrong friends because they're trying to genuinely save them. Unfortunately, not everyone who is at the bottom is willing to rise. Other times, the reason might be of a narcissistic nature; an inflated self-importance that pushes one to interfere in the troubles of another. You cannot compare yourself to Christ who was the standard perfect man. He could hang out with drunkards and prostitutes, but not you. Psychological studies point to the fact that it is easier to pull downward than upward. It might be because appearing to help someone else makes you look good or feel better about your own shortcomings. In other cases, not everyone who is down is ready to accept help. In fact, it is best to see the troubled person make an effort to be better before intervening. And even at that, you must be careful not to sink yourself. This doesn't justify deserting someone in real need to pursue your narrow ambition though.

Remember this: if you won't recommend a particular friend to someone you care about, why hang around the same yourself? You are not obligated to tie yourself to someone who is not willing to be better; not willing to make the world a better place. If you surround yourself with the right people, they will not validate your destructiveness, but will support your upward movement and provide constructive criticism when it is needed. The wrong 'friends', however, will encourage your destructive traits and get jealous when you break out or do something above the rut. Inadvertently, they will tie you down because your progression highlights their faults.

When you dare to break away from the rut and make something meaningful out of yourself, you are indirectly telling them that they are where they are, not because life is so unjust, but because they refuse to rise above the world. Cultivate friendships with those who want the best for you.

RULE 4 COMPARE YOURSELF TO WHO YOU WERE YESTERDAY, NOT TO WHO SOMEONE ELSE IS TODAY

KEY TAKEAWAYS:

- *It is easier than ever to be aware of others' accomplishments*

- *Remember you are you, so don't compare another's achievements with yours*

- *Do a self-audit, making necessary changes and comparing only your yesterday's results to your today's results*

- *Don't be scared to see beyond your normal scope*

The global village in which we live today makes it possible to keep up with the lives- the achievements- of almost every other person on the face of the earth. Our achievements pale in comparison to that of everyone else in the world. You could be enjoying the serotonin-fuelled confidence of your accomplishments in one minute, and in the next, realise there's someone who does way better. This makes the critical, internal voice that resides in each one of us much louder, undermining our efforts. This same voice, although quite necessary for the survival of standards, induces a feeling of worthlessness in one too many people.

The first step to stilling this voice is to accept that "Success" and "Failure" are no Black-or-white concepts. First off, there are more than one games at which one can succeed or fail- Lawyer, Carpenter, Schoolteacher. You can invent your own game. Consider also that it's unlikely you're playing one game at a time; you might be good at some, average at others, and struggling with the rest. And just the same way, you might be better at some games than another person who is better than you at other games.

Ultimately, our lives as adults are more personalized, bearing peculiar situations. We are no longer kids who have yet to undertake much in life, and so look to others as a standard. As human beings, we are always aiming; ever gunning for a better future than our inadequate present. While this attribute helps us to seek new ways of doing things and improve the world, it can also result in chronic agitation and discomfort, an obsessive compulsion to do better. So how do you strike a balance?

First off, take an inventory of your life so far. That critical inside voice can help you in doing this, but make sure not to let it run off. Make a list of the things you **could**, and **would** change. Start small.

Acknowledge and reward it when you keep to your word on the slightest changes. Do this daily, comparing only your personal, peculiar yesterday to your personal, peculiar today. Stay consistent, and your sight will begin to receive focus, because what you aim at determines what you see.

Psychological studies and demonstrations have proven that most of us only see within the scope of what we aim at. There is so much more in the world that we cannot afford to see everything, but then, when we face an obstacle, that restrictiveness can have us in a rut. The good thing also is that, there is so much opportunity out there that we're not taking advantage of. Not getting what we want can push us to see outside our limited frame and force us to grow.

This is the crux of the matter. What you aim at will determine what the universe makes available to your sight; what you see. In all, remember you are a peculiar being. None other is like you. So compare yourself only to who you were yesterday, not to what someone else is today.

RULE 5 DO NOT LET YOUR CHILDREN DO ANYTHING THAT MAKES YOU DISLIKE THEM

KEY TAKEAWAYS:

- *It is every parent's duty to make their children socially desirable*

- *Children also have innate evil, just as they have innate goo*

- *Discipline is a responsibility of parents to children; there must be rules*

- *Use the least amount of force to enforce the rule*

- *Parents must not fail to discipline because they're scared of hatred from the kids*

I have seen parents lose their freedom because they couldn't take the time to let their children know what is not okay. They instead micromanage these children, watching obsessively over them to avoid any self-harm as a result of their awful behaviour. I have seen women who advocate gender equality display obvious preferential treatment for their sons. Apart from cultural preferences, one possible psycho-biological reason for that male preference could be the fact that a male child offers more possibility of a longer lineage, at least in the days before birth control.

My clinical clients often come to me with challenges they're experiencing with their children. One particular one has been spending a ridiculous amount of time struggling to put an uncooperative son to bed. Modern trends in attributing who and who are guilty in such situations is alarming. One of such is the erroneous belief- however idealistic- that children can do no wrong; that it is always the parent's fault. Parents are now extremely cautious not to hurt their children's sensitivities and have abandoned their roles as disciplinary agents. But children are human, and every human possesses innate tendencies for good and evil.

Primatologist Jane Goodall, also established through her work that society and history cannot be blamed exclusively for the evil in man. As such, children cannot be left to their own devices and expected to grow into well-rounded adults. Parents need to pay the right attention- informing them; disciplining them; encouraging them- to their children, else they'll grow into needy, attention-seeking adults- whom nobody likes to hang around.

Most parents get it wrong because they want their kids to see them as friends; to like them. But that is not a parent's role. A child will have many friends but only two parents. It is up to you to train the child such that they will be able to have meaningful interactions with society. For other parents, they'd rather avoid the work involved in disciplining their kids. Discipline them, and when you see a compliance to your discipline, reward such behaviour. Part of disciplining is studying your child to know what works best, because every child is unique. Often, today's parents are scared of crossing the line between Discipline and Punishment, but you can go beyond that barrier by adhering to two general principles of discipline:

- Limit the rules
- Use the least force necessary to enforce those rules
- Discipline is likely to be more effective when parents come in pairs
- Parents should understand their own capacity to be harsh, vengeful, arrogant, resentful, angry and deceitful, so that they don't damage a child in the name of discipline.

- Parents must realize it is their responsibility to act as representations for the real world. It's a chaotic world out there and it's up to parents to prepare their kids; make them socially competent and desirable.

RULE 6 SET YOUR HOUSE IN PERFECT ORDER BEFORE YOU CRITICIZE THE WORLD

KEY TAKEAWAYS:

- *Your reaction towards tragedy and suffering is very important*

- *You can either choose to take responsibility for your life or become vengeful, hurting more people in retaliation*

- *Bad things happen when we hold the rules in contempt and let corruption run free*

One of the most common reactions we have to deep pain or horror is to question Being and express a total disenchantment with existence, "Why must innocent people suffer so terribly? What kind of bloody, horrible planet is this, anyway?" Truly, the world can seem an unfair place. Regardless of how good or bad we are, it

35

appears we're all doomed to certain fates- sickness, death. Whether you believe these global unpleasant events are God's fault, or fate's or yours, what matters most is what you do about them, or rather, what you let them do to you. You can choose to be like Carl Panzram, the sexually abused and damaged kid who grew to become one of the most vengeful murderers of the twentieth century, or like Aleksandr Solzhenitsyn who, while suffering from cancer in a soviet labour camp, channelled his travails to writing the ground-breaking book that would shatter the façade of communism.

There are people who refuse to judge reality or blame God when bad things happen. Take the biblical record of the Hebrew children for example. God made a covenant with them; He chose them and blessed them. They prospered. Then they began to forget their end of the bargain. Corruption prevailed. They grew complacent with the rules and the attendant result was God smiting them. And this is exactly what happens. We grow complacent with rules and then complain when the results hit. In the same way, the New Orleans hurricane could have been prevented if the Flood Control Act of 1965 was judiciously carried out. Yes, a hurricane is an act of God, but failure to do the needful on our part, is sin. And even the Bible says the wages of sin is death. If we decide to heap all the blame for our suffering on Being or God, we tend to sink faster in the mire of bitterness and thirst for retaliation. If you notice your mind is becoming poisoned as a result of your suffering, pause to ask yourself, "Have I cleaned up my life? Have I set my house in order before attempting to fit the world into a box?" Is there anything you know you can do right now to make things better? Things you need to say. Habits you need to stop. Opportunities you can grab. Anything that will alleviate your suffering at all.

When you consistently stop doing what is wrong, you're taking charge of your existence. Instinctively, your soul knows what is wrong for it. You can take pointers from culture and past experience, but don't let it overrule your judgment. Steadily, you are uncluttering your soul of the bitterness and resentment. You will soon find that you're capable of seeing the world in better light. You'll become strong enough to handle those inevitable tragedies- like death- that all mankind has to deal with. Then, you'll possibly see your soul's existence as a genuine good, as something to celebrate, even in the face of your own vulnerability.

RULE 7 PURSUE WHAT IS MEANINGFUL (NOT WHAT IS EXPEDIENT)

KEY TAKEAWAYS:

- *Man's awareness of his ability to hurt another for the sake of suffering is greater than the tragedy of life*

- *The pursuit of instant pleasure, though tempting, does not make for the ultimate fulfilment*

The fact that suffering is a part of life and that death is inevitable prompts a sort of instinctive response- the pursuit of pleasure regardless of consequences. Do whatever makes you happy, no matter how insignificant or dangerous. After all, we're all going to suffer and die anyway. Or what else could be done?

Answers lie in ancestral treasures which we have weaved into stories and rituals, but fail to consider. Like the biblical record of Paradise and the Fall of man. Following the disobedience to God and consequent fall from perfection, the idea of sacrifice came into play, with our forefathers- as with Cain and Abel- struggling, hoping to gain God's favour and appease his wrath. Sacrifice entails giving up something now for something better in the future; delayed gratification. It is work. Small sacrifices can solve small, simple problems but larger sacrifices will be required to guarantee a solution of larger consequence down the line in the future.

The Cain and Abel story also imply that not all sacrifices are of equal quality, and that some of seemingly high quality are not rewarded with a better future- and it's not clear why. Over the years, with carefully observed patterns, man has come to realise that delaying our pleasure can be rewarding. But then, as in the case of biblical Abraham, it would seem God revels in asking for the very best. That was baffling. Why did he keep asking for more? This can be a useful analogy in understanding how life works. Sometimes, when we want a better situation, we need to sacrifice some more, possibly what we love best. We need to be able to let go.

But what exactly is the ultimate sacrifice? It is depicted by God's sacrifice of Christ Jesus, His son. It is the sacrifice of self and child, and ancient Greek philosopher, Socrates also exemplified this when he, facing execution, willingly gave up his life. He accepted the inevitability of man's end and recounting that he had lived a meaningful life, did not despair to depart the world. We learn from his existence that "if you abide, truthfully and courageously, by the highest of ideals, you will be provided with more security and strength than will be offered by any short-sighted concentration on your own safety; if you live properly, fully, you can discover meaning so profound that it protects you even from the fear of death."

But tragedy is not the only thing that makes us suffer. Our self-consciousness (thanks to Adam and Eve) has made us acutely aware of our capacity for evil. We know we can hurt another just for the sake of hurting. And when our sacrifices don't produce the desired results- as with Cain and Abel- we can take it out on those whose sacrifices do. Evil greatly multiplies the suffering of man on earth and elicits more of that expedient, immediate pleasure kind of reaction. The kind of sacrifice that is required to overcome evil is a question that has been pondered in the Christian sphere, and elsewhere, for centuries. If the worst sin is the act of inflicting torment on others, just for the sake of it, then it figures that consciously alleviating unnecessary pain and suffering is good. You cannot do this by being expedient. There is no sacrifice in expediency. To have meaning, and to follow it, is the ultimate sacrifice. "Meaning is the Way, the path of life more abundant, the place you live when you are guided by Love and speaking Truth and when nothing you want or could possibly want takes any precedence over precisely that."

RULE 8 TELL THE TRUTH— OR, AT LEAST, DON'T LIE

KEY TAKEAWAYS:

- *A lie can get you what you want now, but it is only temporary*

- *Lies and deceit are at the bottom of everything that ails man*

- *Speaking and living your truth sets you free*

While training to become a clinical psychologist, I once encountered a schizophrenic woman at Montreal's Douglas Hospital. She had asked my colleague if she could join our group, and when my colleague asked what she should say- trying to avoid hurting the patient's feelings- I simply told her the truth; that we were training to be psychologists and so she couldn't join our group. Earlier on, I had become aware of my tendency to speak untruths in the bid to get something, and I had taken conscious efforts to speak truth always, or at least not tell a lie. This came in handy when I had a paranoid patient, as well as with my alcoholic landlord who kept trying to sell me things to fuel his habit. The truth is usually not the easy way out.

It is possible to manipulate situations with words to get what you want; to live a life-lie. One of the dangers here is that when you speak the lie often enough, you start to believe it, patterning your life after something untrue and unlikely to happen. The end is always nothing short of a disaster. Another dangerous perspective of the life-lie is avoidance. Choosing to remain 'safe' and telling yourself everything is perfect stunts self-realization and results in an incomplete being. Living a lie is deliberately closing your eyes to the truth, no matter how unpleasant. The more the lies, the more difficult it is to adjust to the truth when it comes, because eventually, it will catch up with you.

When you're living a lie, you refuse to take responsibility for failures, instead placing it on society, Being, etc. It's only a short walk from here to "They should be punished for this", unleashing evil. Someone makes a new, unproductive rule at work, but you'd rather pretend it's okay than admit how misplaced it is. Lies have been found to be at the bottom of everything that ails man- physically, psychologically, spiritually. It tears at the fabric of any family unit that entertains it, and in extension, society. The more humans damaged by lies and deceit, the more damaged the world is. But if we resort to honesty, even though we might not be able to make this earth a paradise, we will definitely be able to reduce the suffering inherent within.

Having an aim implies that one looks into the future and make projections; map out routes and decisions. To avoid falling into totalitarian certainty, one can look to culture; how things have been ordered so far. This does not mean discarding one's peculiarities however. Christ is often referred to as Logos, the Word of God which created order from chaos at the beginning of time, and eventually sacrificed itself, in human form, for all mankind. "Every bit of new information challenges a previous conception, forcing it to dissolve into chaos before it can be reborn as something better." Be consciously aware of your speech and actions. Soon enough, you will be able to identify distinct markers that will tell you when you're lying, and you can start eliminating it little by little. Telling your truth will bring order into your chaos. Accept your truth and tell it, because nobody knows it like you do. Live it also. You may not like the initial results because, of course, it's not the easy way out. It may not get you what you want instantly- and temporarily- as the lies. But it will free you, and open you up to a light that will keep burning even as your soul comes upon life's catastrophes. It will also keep you from transferring blame and seeking vengeance. Speaking and living your truth is the closest you'll ever get to Paradise.

RULE 9 ASSUME THAT THE PERSON YOU ARE LISTENING TO MIGHT KNOW SOMETHING YOU DON'T

KEY TAKEAWAYS:

- *Conversations come in various forms and each has an ultimate goal*

- *Psychotherapy involves active listening*

- *People talk to organize their thoughts and find meaning amidst their chaotic experiences*

- *The highest form of conversation is one in which all participants are open to learning form one another*

Psychotherapy, unlike advice, is sincere conversation-listening more than talking. I have learnt very surprising things from my clinical patients by really listening to them. In fact, some reveal their diagnosis and treatment if you listen well enough. I once had a client who thought she had been raped a couple of times. Instead of suggesting plausible explanations and creating theories from all the information she'd given me concerning the incidents, I chose to listen. I listen because talking is how people usually think. Thinking, in the real sense of the word involves conversation between two or more of yourself. It involves creating avatars of yourself in a fictional world to dissect issues. But the process is quite emotionally excruciating and physiologically challenging that people would rather talk. When people talk to a listening person, they get the effect of interacting with common humanity. The listening person does this by not talking and giving the speaker free rein to talk to themselves. As much as it is important to give people their space to talk, you must be careful not to appear detached. Participate with the subtlest of cues to communicate that you're a part of the psychotherapeutic process.

Bottom-line: You both tell each other the truth. You both listen. But listening is never as easy as it seems, and a lot of people don't get it. Carl Rogers suggests taking time to summarize what the other person has said, and only if that person agrees with your summary, is it valid. The first obvious advantage to this is that you're sure you *really* understand what the person is saying, and not just projecting your own meaning. Also, it puts the narrated experience more compactly, such that the client grasps a better understanding of the events. The result is that such a client sees more clearly, identifies where he made mistakes, and what to do to correct and/or avoid the same next time. Lastly, this approach makes it very unlikely that you'll raise irrelevant, straw man arguments against a person's narrated experience.

Sometimes, talking is not for the sake of thinking and listening is not considered in a conversation. Usually, such conversations, of different variants, involve one person trying to enthrone his or her ideas as supreme and claim the top position. Political and economic conversations usually follow this pattern, with each speaker trying to assert the dominance of his side without bothering to listen to the others. In a true listening conversation, the speaker is allowed to let it all out; organize all the chaos in his/her mind by putting them into words, not minding the straying every now and then.

These conversations sometimes result in conflict between men and women because both sexes are typically focused on different things. While men tend to emphasize fixing things, women are more concerned with verbalizing the problem correctly. If both sides can see that the other's position is valid and useful, then much headway can be made. Other conversational types include lectures where a speaker speaks to people that mostly respond non-verbally, and witty exchanges, which is more common among people who share close bonds and the goal is usually to be the most entertaining speaker of the lot.

Another form of conversation is one in which all the parties involved are participating. Mutual exploration is the foundation as both parties listen for the sake of knowing, learning, considering the unknown (Chaos) while living in the known (order). The ultimate goal here is not to dominate, convince, oppress or entertain. As such, each speaker listens to and respects the personal leanings of the others. You cannot achieve this type of conversation if you're comfortable with living in your lie; resistant to change. In the end, wisdom is not resident in the knowledge you already possess, but in your continual search for more. To attain this height, always assume that everyone you're speaking with has new knowledge from which you can be informed.

RULE 10 BE PRECISE IN YOUR SPEECH

KEY TAKEAWAYS:

- *We typically do not perceive beyond the context of our immediate realities*

- *The existence of chaos elicits discomfort in our lives*

- *It is important not to ignore chaotic realities in a bid to avoid discomfort*

- *Ignored chaotic situations will eventually pile up and return with a propensity to crush*

- *Articulate any existing chaos, and map out a precise solution*

- *Use precise language*

We see things in context of their use their value. In this way, we don't just see a floor as what it is. We perceive it as something to walk on. We see rocks because we can throw them; we see chairs to sit on them. In this way, we see everything in the world through the lens of our precise, often narrow purpose.

Take our laptops for example. It goes beyond the black box we can see. In fact, what makes it functional is an interconnectedness between it and other parts housed within. Once those parts become non-existent, our laptops become little more than museum relics. We don't see the world in things and objects. We are wired to see everything within it as something to utilize; something to assist us in achieving our aim. Like when we see other human beings, we don't see the complex system of organs, cells, and molecules within them. We don't see their interconnectedness with family and friends. All these things combine to make them who they really are, but we do not see all that. We only see that we need to communicate with the particular person and only at that particular time.

This singleness- precision- of our aim is what keeps us from getting lost in the world's largeness. We have the ability to extend our personal boundaries to conform to the different situations we find ourselves. That is why we can see ourselves variously as parent, child, boss, employee, car owner, patriot, etc. as the situation demands it. It can be quite demanding to understand the chaotic interconnectedness of our realities and that awareness only comes when our order is threatened.

For instance, we see a car as nothing beyond that which transports us, but once that car develops a fault, or does not function as it is supposed to, we become more aware of its interconnectedness within its parts. All those things which were a part of the world's reality, but excluded from our precise reality- would now find their way into our perceptual frame.

The absence of precision, in essence, brings chaos. When things fall apart, we lose sight of the order and gain sight of the chaos. We are thrown into a state of emergency by what we did not expect. Often times however, the chaos that finally got our attention has been preceded by signs; mini-chaos that we preferred not to be articulate or precise about because it would mean admitting a less-than-perfect situation. So when we are hit by the rubbish heap that we've let pile up, we give in to ancient reflexive responses.

But the prevention can still be the cure. All parties involved must be ready to stop living a lie, articulate the existing chaos, and map out a precise solution. Avoiding our chaos only perpetuates, and sometimes increases, that chaos. If you shy away from confronting unexpected realities head-on, reality itself becomes increasingly chaotic. Your language matters a lot. Stop lying to yourself and to others. Exercise caution with your words; what you say about the actions you've taken, the decisions you're making, and where you're headed. It is possible to reorganize the chaotic past by reducing it- using precise language- to its essence.

It is precision that gives you a clearer perception of your situation, making it possible to create a new order from that chaos.

RULE 11 DO NOT BOTHER CHILDREN WHEN THEY ARE SKATEBOARDING

KEY TAKEAWAYS:

- *There can be no real growth without risks and anything that says otherwise is anti-human*

Human beings are wired with a thrill for danger. We don't want danger enough to destroy us, but we welcome- some more than others- danger to challenge us. When human beings overprotected and kept too safe, we begin to look out for ways to make things dangerous because when we succeed in spite of danger, we feel accomplished and competent. So when a university management installs skate stoppers on their property to prevent a group of boys from skating, they're indirectly denying them that sense of accomplishment. And as psychologists, Freud, Jung, and Nietzsche put forth, there is a dark side to everything. Could the rules applied to stop the boys from engaging in highly skilled, courageous, and dangerous activity be rooted in a sinister and extremely anti-human spirit?

My friend Chris, had that same spirit. Plagued with feelings of guilt- about life's unfairness- from his childhood, he trudged along life with a bitterness for masculinity, masculine activity, and eventually, all human. He turned his back on education or any form of ambition and engaged in self-destructive activities. His soul darkened with each passing day and eventually, at the sight of what looked like his life was going to be meaningful, he committed suicide. He probably did not think he deserved any form of good coming his way.

Humans are a very peculiar specie. Asides from the fact that they have no equal, they do not appear to have any limits. Feats that were termed impossible many years back have become common activity today. But there are members of this race who have appointed themselves judges and proceed to mete out judgment. The most extreme forms of this judgment has included shootings and mass murders. In modern world, these planet defenders still exist, criticizing others simply because they belong to the human species. The boys suffer it more, as it appears societal structure is tilted towards setting them up for failure, whichever way. One of the obvious disparities is in Education. In the next 15 years, there will be very many educated women and very *very* few educated men. This is as much a problem for the men as it is for women who usually prefer a partner of equal or greater socio-economic status. But today, political correctness is permeating schools- and every other social institution- and fuelling oppression and hostility towards men, even when history proves that the idea of male oppression is faulty. These leanings are mostly drawn from Marxist ideologies.

Some schools of thought advocate that boys be socialized the same way as girls. They believe this will help put an end to male aggression which, in their estimation, is taught as part of a male socialization routine of sorts. They forget that aggression is not taught. It is innate. Most aggressive 2-year olds, by the time they're four, have been socialized to realize that such aggressive tendencies are unacceptable in the world. Asides this, aggression in itself is not entirely evil, as most of my female clients have their problems rooted, not in over-aggressiveness, but in the fact that they are not aggressive enough. A healthy form of aggression is needed for self-protection as an overly agreeable female is prime target for bullying.

Despite idealistic arguments against male aggressiveness, there are still certain standards upheld, interestingly by both sexes. Men typically demand toughness from each other. Nobody wants to hear you whining when there's work to be done. You must be able to stand it when you're being tested: how much exactly can you take? You need to be able to rise up to life's challenges. Women, also typically want a strong man. They do not want an additional child. They want someone they can rely on. So why try to scrap the process through which boys become men? The spirit that hinders the progression of humans- not just men- from child to adult is something to be opposed. If you're of the opinion that tough men are dangerous, try pitching your tent with a weak man and you'll be horrified. There can be no real growth without risks and anything that says otherwise is anti-human.

RULE 12 PET A CAT WHEN YOU ENCOUNTER ONE ON THE STREET

KEY TAKEAWAYS:

- *Vulnerability is a part of Being*

- *We love people, not outside their limitations- sickness, character flaw, etc. - but in spite of it*

- *Even in chaos, take time to pause and smell the roses*

If we have come to know the inevitability of suffering in life, how possible is it to cope or even be happy in the face of such grim facts? I was speaking with a client recently. Her husband had been winning a 5-year battle with cancer. Until now. He had been given how much time he had left, and to say the least, his wife was devastated. She was asking the same questions every other person asks in such situations: Why him?

When my son, Julian, was younger, I thought often about how fragile he was and how he could easily be hurt. I thought of how I would 'fix' him to be stronger, if only I had the power. But I also realised that then he would no longer be the Julian I love so much. I realised that vulnerability is a part of Being. If we are have no limitations, no imperfections, then the whole essence of Being- or Becoming- is defeated. We can see this play out in the storyline of every superhero character in pop culture. Superman has Kryptonite.

My daughter, Mikhaila, not much older, was the most cheerful child. Yet, at the age of 6, she was diagnosed with arthritis. It was not the easiest thing to watch your child suffer and I doubted the reason for any existence at all. This line of thought, quite instinctive, when acted upon, becomes the underlying principle for suicides and genocides.

Awareness of the limitations inherent in existence will not make the suffering go away, but it will help us notice that we love people, not outside their limitations- sickness, character flaw, etc. - but in spite of it. Because after all, we cannot separate one from the other. More importantly, this awareness can only prove useful in moments of pain and suffering, if the people involved can see the good in existence. Faith in Being propels you to make the best of your chaos, as we learned while dealing with our daughter, Mikhaila's arthritis.

- Set aside time every day to talk and think about the chaotic situation and how it should be managed every day.

- Save your strength. Refuse to be overwhelmed by worries.

- Don't think about the situation close to bedtime. You need all the sleep you can get during such periods.

- Stay positive. As much as you can, keep a sunny disposition.

The ability to see the good in existence matters a lot. If people lose that basic faith- in Being, in humanity- then they are truly lost.

Like cats, which are typically not social, but might once in a while let you pet them or play around with your dog, there is some light to be seen even in the darkest situations. While going through the pain and suffering attendant of Being, take the time to be aware of life's sunny rays- a little girl dancing on the street; good coffee in a café with great customer service. Steal some time amidst the chaos to do something ridiculous that can make you forget temporarily, the horrors of existence. You may not normally be drawn to pet a cat, but when you encounter one, please do.